Koblenz was founded by the Romans, making it one of the oldest cities in Germany. Its location where the Moselle flows into the Rhine is unique, and also gives the city its name. The Romans called in 'Confluentes' (= confluence), and this lives on in the German name, which until 1926 was officially spelt 'Coblenz'. Large areas of the city are part of the 'Upper Middle Rhine Valley' UNESCO World Heritage Site. An unusual manmade landscape with castles and churches in the midst of enchanting countryside has been preserved here. With more than 100,000 inhabitants, Koblenz is today more than just a supraregional centre. It is also home to a university, and to the German Federal Archive, as well as the headquarters of two federal agencies, the Federal Office for Defence Technology and Procurement, and the Federal Office for Military Information Management and Information Technology.

Burg Stolzenfels, one of the best-known castles on the Rhine, stands just a few kilometres to the south of Koblenz

History

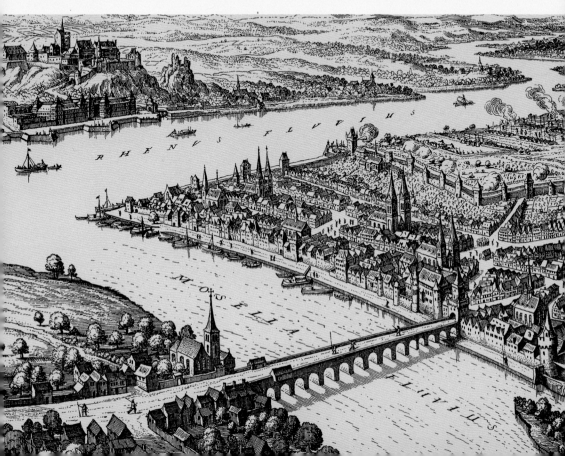

Koblenz was built shortly after the birth of Christ as a citadel to secure the place where the road from Mainz to Cologne crossed the Moselle. The pile bridge over the river was situated 50 metres downstream of the present-day Balduin Bridge. The citadel stood, as recent excavations have shown, in the vicinity of St Castor's church, i.e. at the confluence of the Rhine and the Moselle. The Roman fortress measured app. 100 x 100 metres and was surrounded by a ditch 4 metres across and 2.5 metres deep. Some 1,000 soldiers were stationed here with the job of securing the frontier of the empire, which at this point was formed by the Rhine. To the west of the citadel a flourishing Roman trading town grew up on the Moselle, for which in addition to the above-mentioned bridge

across the Moselle, a further wooden bridge over the Rhine was built a little later. After attacks by the Germanic tribes, the town was given a permanent wall in about 300 AD. This late Roman fortification, which included 19 round towers, each with a diameter of 10 metres, is still extant in a number of places and has been integrated into subsequent buildings.

Even after the collapse of the Roman Empire, Koblenz retained its supraregional importance as a royal seat of the Franks from the fifth century. In the Middle Ages the collegiate church of St Castor, consecrated in 836, became an important cultural centre. It was here in 842 that the negotiations between Charlemagne's three grandsons took place, leading to the division of the Frankish Empire in the Treaty of Verdun in 843.

Portal dating from 1754/1967 of the Dominican priory, founded c. 1230, destroyed in 1944 and not rebuilt

Koblenz 1632 (during the siege by the Swedes in the Thirty Years' War), view by Merian, 1646

In 1018 Emperor Henry II donated the revenues from Koblenz to the Archbishop of Trier. As the city was significant both economically and strategically, this marked the start of the rule of the archbishops of Trier on this section of the Rhine, which was to last until the French Revolution. In about 1000, a castle was built on the rocky outcrop known as Ehrenbreitstein, which over the centuries was continually expanded into a major fortress. It was used as a depository for important sacred items in unsettled times. The Elector Archbishops of Trier also erected a further castle, Stolzenfels, to the south of the city as a customs post; and to defend themselves against the increasingly rebellious citizenry, they also built the Alte Burg, or 'old castle'. In the early thirteenth century the Teutonic Knights (1216), the Dominicans (c. 1230) and the Franciscans (1236) all built priories in the city. However it was not until the four-

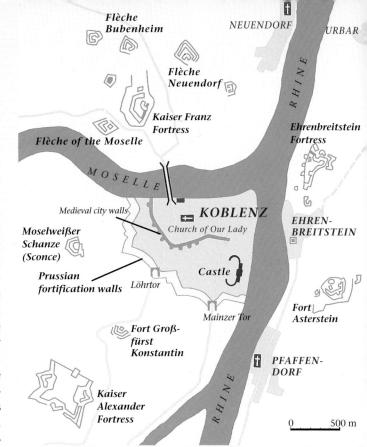

teenth century that the Balduin Bridge, the first fixed Moselle crossing since Roman times, was built.

In the fifteenth century, the collegiate churches of St Castor and St Florinus became centres of eminent scholarly activity that left their mark Europe-wide, with such notable personalities as Winand von Steeg and Nicholas of Cusa. At the Reformation Koblenz remained Catholic. During the Thirty

Koblenz with its major fortresses, 1840 (after H. Fischer/ A. Müller 2002)

Fort Asterstein in Ehrenbreitstein dating from 1818–28

View of Koblenz from Ehrenbreitstein

Years' War, Archbishop-Elector Philipp Christoph von Sötern moved his residence from Trier to the newly erected Philippsburg Palace beneath Ehrenbreitstein Fortress.

Since the seventeenth century, Koblenz's favourable location in terms of transport routes has proved disastrous in times of war. Time and again the city has been fortified, destroyed, slighted and rebuilt, particularly in the Thirty Years' War (1618–48), the War of the Grand Alliance (also known as the War of the Palatine Succession or Nine Years' War, 1688–97), during the period of French occupation (1794–1814) and in the Second World War, when 85 % of the city centre was destroyed.

The occupation of the city by the army of the French Revolution in 1794 represented a major historical caesura. As a result of the secularization of ecclesiastical property throughout the Holy Roman Empire in 1803, all of the city's collegiate churches and priories were dissolved. The agreements reached at the Congress of Vienna in 1815 saw Koblenz handed to the kingdom of Prussia. The city became the seat of government of the province with the

name of 'Grand Duchy of the Lower Rhine', and later the capital of the Prussian Rhine Province; the new masters turned Koblenz into a fortress city with some of the strongest fortifications in Europe.

The first railway reached Koblenz in 1858. Since then, further bridges have been built over the Rhine and Moselle. At the same time, developments in weapons technology were rendering the fortifications obsolete, and in 1890 a start was made on demolishing them. Kaiser Wilhelm I lived in Koblenz with his consort Augusta for a long

time. His memorial was set up on the Deutsches Eck in 1897. The start of the new century saw extensive additions to the city, especially in the south, with some outstanding buildings, including notable churches and the central railway station.

At the end of the Great War, Koblenz was occupied first by American, then by French troops. Then during the Second World War, heavy damage by enemy action radically changed the appearance of the city, although the most important historic buildings were mostly restored.

DEUTSCHHERRENHAUS (House of the Teutonic Knights – Ludwig Museum)

As early as 1216, Archbishop Theoderic II (Dietrich von Wied) invited the knights of the Teutonic Order (Deutscher Orden) to Koblenz and gave them the land at the confluence of the Moselle with the Rhine (now known, after them, as the 'Deutsches Eck') together with the already existing St Nicholas Hospital. This makes Koblenz the oldest seat of the order in the Rhineland. The community was directly subordinate to the Grand Master of the order, and administered numerous of its possessions all the way from Mechelen in Flanders to Mainz. After the destruction suffered by the city in the Second World War, the only parts of the former complex to be restored were the Gothic main building (the 'Rheinbau') dating from 1279, and the cellar of the 'Moselbau' with its groined vault (fourteenth century). Of the church, consecrated in 1306 and destroyed in 1811, remains of the south wall and a chapel erected in 1354/55 on the south side of the choir still survive, albeit as ruins. Also still extant are the fortification walls facing the two rivers, as well as the gatehouse and the Archive Keeper's House of 1895/96 (erected when the complex was rebuilt as a Prussian state archive).

Since 1992 the 'Rheinbau' has housed the Ludwig Museum of contemporary French art, the fifth art museum in Germany to have been established on the initiative of the collectors Peter Ludwig and his wife Irene. Peter Ludwig (1925–96), a chocolate manufacturer based in Aachen, was born in Koblenz.

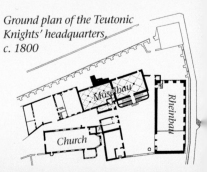

Ground plan of the Teutonic Knights' headquarters, c. 1800

DEUTSCHES ECK

The city's favourable location in terms of transport is most apparent at the 'Deutsches Eck', where the Moselle flows into the Rhine. This tongue of land got its name from the Teutonic Knights (Deutscher Orden), who in 1216 were given land here formerly belonging to the collegiate church of St Castor. The plaza is the location of a memorial to Kaiser Wilhelm I dating from 1897. The original equestrian statue, made of beaten copper plates (damaged and dismantled in 1945, replaced by a cast-bronze replica in 1993), was designed by Emil Hundrieser. The plinth and surrounds were the work of Bruno Schmitz, who also designed the memorial to the Battle of the Nations in Leipzig.

Equestrian statue of Kaiser Wilhelm I on the 'Deutsches Eck'

ST CASTOR

View of St Castor, in the background the church of Our Lady (left) and of St Florinus (right). Since July 2010 the Rhine Cableway – at 890 metres the longest in Germany – has run from the Rhine embankment by St Castor to the plateau of Ehrenbreitstein Fortress. In order not to endanger the UNESCO World Heritage status of the Upper Middle Rhine Valley, the intention is to dismantle the cableway at the end of 2013.

In the early and high Middle Ages, St Castor was the religious and cultural centre of Koblenz, although until the end of the thirteenth century the church was still outside the city walls. Small parts of the original structure are still preserved in the present building. It occupies the site of a Roman ambulatory temple and was consecrated in 836 by Archbishop Hetto in the presence of King Louis the Pious, the day after the relics of St Castor of Karden on the Moselle were translated to the church. The college of canons, dissolved in 1802, was probably in existence even during the foundation phase.

The Carolingian church, dating from before 836, had an aisleless nave, transepts, apse, apse ambulatory, and a round choir at the easternmost point of the latter. This structure still largely determines the dimensions of the present-day building. Some of the original fabric still survives in the foundations, from the transept to the imposts of the choir arches, and probably at the west end too. This latter took on its present-day appearance as a façade with two towers in the first half of the eleventh century. The choir with its two flanking towers was built in the mid-twelfth century. After major damage in 1198 during the war between Philip of Swabia and Emperor Otto IV, a broad, low flat-ceilinged Romanesque nave

top: tomb of Arch-
bishop Kuno von
Falkenstein (d. 1388)
in the blind Gothic
arch in the choir

bottom: tomb of
Archbishop Werner
von Königstein
(d. 1418) in the
ogee arch in the choir

with vaulted aisles was built. The work was completed by the time the church was rededicated in 1208. A little later, the west towers were each given an extra storey and a relatively steep Rhen-ish helm. In the late fifteenth century, the nave was vaulted over, and the crossing was given a rib-vault.

Following the dissolution of 1802, the collegiate buildings and the Ro-

top left:
St Castor, façade

11

manesque gatehouse to the cemetery were demolished. In 1848/49 the Baroque fittings and the choir screen were removed as part of a restoration undertaken by Johann Claudius von Lassaulx. In the early 1850s Joseph A. Settegast painted the interior of the church with large murals, of which, since 1928, only that in the apse survives. When the exterior was restored in 1890–95, the city architect F. W. Maeckler renewed the south aisle and the south sacristy. During the Second World War, the roofs and the organ were destroyed.

Ground plan after Krause 1920
black = before 836   choir = c. 1150/60
nave = before 1208

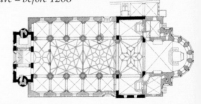

*top: St Castor,
view from the south*

*left: the building
erected in 1835 as a
girls' school for the
parish of St Castor to
designs by the impor-
tant architect Johann
Claudius von Lassaulx
in the round-arch
style (altered in the
attic storey in
1912/13) served as
the Rhine Museum
from 1911 to 1944*

*left: presbytery of
St Castor, built in
1830 in the round-
arch style to designs
by Johann Claudius
von Lassaulx*

left: St Castor, pulpit dating from 1625

13

ST JAMES'S CHAPEL/VON-DER-LEYENSCHER-HOF

Castor Fountain, commemorating Napoleon's Russian campaign of 1812, originally surmounted by the statues of Father Rhine and Mother Moselle

Memorial to Peter Altmeier (1899–1977), first elected state premier of Rhineland-Palatinate 1947–69

In the grounds of the former Von der Leyenscher Hof (Kastorstrasse 2, today the State Office for Roads and Transport), on what used to be the Teutonic Knights' cemetery, stands the Gothic St James's Chapel, built in 1355 and now used by the Old Catholic congregation. Together with an adjacent building, its exterior was refashioned in around 1725 by the archiepiscopal court architect Johannes Seiz to create a Baroque show façade (originally this was the garden front). It is now the only surviving part of the old Von der Leyenscher Hof complex, which was built by Archbishop Johann von der Leyen (1556–67) as a town house for his family, and enlarged and remodelled several times. The new building on the site dates from 1967.

GÖRRESHAUS

The originally detached Görreshaus (today in the rear courtyard at Eltzerhofstrasse 6, dating from 1892/93) was built as the assembly room of the Catholic Reading Circle formed in 1863, and named after the Catholic publicist Josef Görres (1776–1848). The neo-Gothic building, dating from 1865, with its large hall, is now the home of the Rhineland Palatinate state orchestra, the Rheinische Philharmonie.

Görreshaus (Eltzerhofstrasse 6, rear courtyard)

'DEUTSCHER KAISER'

What was to become the 'Deutscher Kaiser' inn (Kastorstrasse 3) is one of the few medieval houses in Koblenz to have survived the bombardment by the French in 1688. The striking, tower-like building with its battlements was built by the master of the archiepiscopal mint, Konrad von Lengenfeld (d. 1520), in about 1490. The coat of arms of the Lengenfeld family is depicted on the keystone of the star-ribbed vault on the ground floor and in the arcade frieze of the north façade.

PFARRHOF LIEBFRAUEN

The premises at Florinspfaffengasse 14 may go back to the Merovingian royal palace, but there is no conclusive evidence. The two towers with Baroque helms dating from 1701/02

St James's Chapel

top left: 'Deutscher Kaiser'
top right: Grocers' Guild House, Korn-
pfortstrasse 17, 1708–10

(reconstructed in 1987) are towers of the late-Roman city wall. In the Middle Ages, the building was an archiepiscopal residence, and also contained a courtroom. It was given its present form in 1680–82 and 1701/02 by Johann Christoph Sabastiani. The gate, dating from 1745, was taken from the Bassenheimer Hof on Balduin Bridge, destroyed in 1944.

Weinhaus Hubertus on Florinsmarkt, timber-framed building dating from c. 1695

top: Eltz-Rübenacher Hof, Kornpfortstrasse 15, today the municipal library, exterior design c. 1701 by Johann Christoph Sebastiani
bottom: Pfarrhof Liebfrauen, Florinspfaffengasse 14

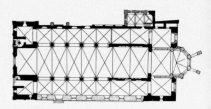

nave vaulted over by Master Dietrich; the vault was rebuilt in 1706–11 after the bombardment by the French in 1688. The priory was dissolved in 1803, when the occupying French forces sold the furniture and fittings; in 1807–11 they went on to demolish the adjacent priory buildings, so that only the Romanesque chapter house and small parts of the cloister (both c. 1200) remained. Following the expulsion of the French, the church was restored for use by the Protestant congregation (from 1818). The tower spires were refashioned in 1899.

The historic fittings have been almost entirely lost. Notable, however, are the medieval glass panes taken

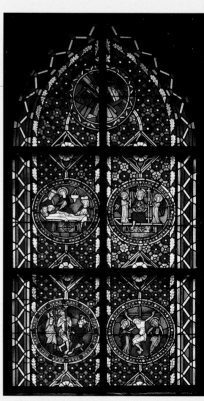

ST FLORINUS

top: St Florinus, façade and ground plan

right: window, round panes with the depiction of the childhood and Passion of Christ, c. 1330, otherwise 1899

The former Augustinian priory church of St Florinus has its origins in the chapel of the neighbouring palace of the Frankish kings. The present church was built as a Romanesque basilica in around 1100, the choir being rebuilt in the Gothic style in the mid-fourteenth century. The church was, to start with, flat-ceilinged throughout. Only between 1582 and 1614 was the

top: St Flori-
nus, view
down the nave
to the choir

left and
bottom centre:
chapter house,
view and
section

far right:
memorial to
Nicolas of Cusa
(1401– 64)
outside the
church – fa-
mous philoso-
pher, theologian
and mathe-
matician, from
1430 dean of
St Florinus,
later also car-
dinal

probably from the church in Dause-
nau, and assembled into large windows in 1899. They show depictions
from the childhood and Passion of
Christ (c. 1330); other windows
show the Crucifixion and Ascension
(these latter probably from Arnstein
Abbey, mid-fourteenth century).

ALTES KAUFHAUS
(Middle Rhine Museum)

The building, erected on Florinsmarkt in 1419–25 as a civic centre ('**Kauf-und Danzhaus**'), served as the City Hall from 1674 to 1794. After suffering damage in the War of the Grand Alliance in 1688, it was given a Baroque mansard roof by Johann Georg Judas, as well as the clock tower with the grimacing head of the 'Eye Roller'. Destroyed in 1944 and rebuilt in 1961/62, the building now houses the **Middle Rhine Museum**, a collection of art from the region (including noteworthy Gothic sculptures and 'Rhine Romantic' paintings). At present undergoing general refurbishment, due to end in 2013, the museum is currently presenting temporary exhibitions. Part of the museum is housed in the Gothic '**Schöffenhaus**' or courthouse, dating from 1528–30 (rebuilt in 1965) with its filigree corner turrets. This was the meeting-place of the 14 'Schöffen', or jurors, who formed the municipal court.

The **Bürresheimer Hof**, dating from 1659/60, with its striking multi-cambered gable, houses the music and young people's libraries. From 1847 to 1938, the building was a synagogue. Between it an the Moselle is the Baroque **Galeriebau** (1771–74) by Nikolaus Lauxen.

ALTE BURG ('OLD CASTLE')

The Alte Burg (now the city archive) stands next to Balduin Bridge, the medieval bridge across the Moselle. Until the construction of the electoral palace in Ehrenbreitstein in the seventeenth century, the archbishops of Trier used it as a seat of government. The complex included a number of utility buildings (stables, slaughterhouse, cowsheds), which over the past 200 years were gradually demolished, so that now only the main building survives. In addition, the area was surrounded on three sides by a wall and a 15–20-metre-wide ditch, which is still extant on the east side.

The castle has its origins in a building erected in around 1185 as the seat of a castellan. It was enlarged by Archbishop Heinrich von Vinstingen (1260–86). This original building had two storeys and reached up to the frieze of round arches which still survives on the façade between the towers. Archbishop Otto von Ziegenhain (1418–30) built the octagonal chapel with Gothic tracery windows on top of the lower part of the east tower, which dates from Roman times, and added the west tower, which at first was detached. The east wing and the staircase tower with its elaborate Renaissance ornamentation date from the time of Archbishop Johann von der Leyen (1556–67). The building took on its present form (west wing, pitched roof, cupolas on the towers) in about 1680–82.

top: Alte Burg, exterior and interior views

bottom: Balduin Bridge, 246 m stone arch bridge over the Moselle, built under Elector Balduin of Luxembourg from c. 1342/43, destroyed by retreating German troops in 1945, rebuilt by 1949, by 1975 five of the original 14 arches had been replaced to facilitate navigation

top: Münzplatz, Art Nouveau murals by William Straube (1911) with the depiction of paradise (left), Metternicher Hof (centre), Market Woman & Policeman and „Resche Hennerich" (bronze figures by Fritz Berlin, top right), Mint Master's House (right)

MÜNZPLATZ ('MINT SQUARE')

The Münzplatz was created as a result of the demolition of the Electoral Mint, which was closed in 1773. While the workshops (kiln, striking shop, etc.) disappeared after 1806, the now detached **Mint Master's House** survives. Built by Johann Seiz in 1761/63, it was where Mint Master Meydinger lived.

Opposite is the **Metternicher Hof**, the townhouse of the barons of Metternich-Winneburg. The structure of the building is medieval, but it was given its present façade in 1674. It was the birthplace of Clemens Wenzeslaus von Metternich (1773–1859), the future Austrian Chancellor and Foreign Minister.

left: intersection of Marktstrasse/Am Plan – four houses dating from 1608 with elaborate oriel towers, restored in 1689–92 by Johann Christoph Sebastiani (after destruction in 1688), Marktstr. 2 and Am Plan 2 given additional storeys in 1862/63, the latter destroyed in 1944, rebuilt in 1950

AM PLAN

top: Am Plan

Am Plan (i. e. 'on the open space') is the location of the north row of houses on the Roman city wall: in the middle is the former **local army command**, with its imposing flight of steps (built in 1719–22 by Johann Georg Judas, served as City Hall 1805–95), to the right, the **former school** (built from 1776 by Nikolaus Lauxen, dormers from 1911/12), and the **Drouvensches Haus** (1779 by Christian Trosson). The fountain dates from 1806 and was built with stones taken from Schönbornlust hunting lodge (1748–52) in nearby Kesselheim, which was destroyed by French troops in 1795.

bottom left: St Michael's Chapel, 13th/14th c., built on the Roman wall, refashioned in the Baroque style 1660, portal with Archangel Michael, 1752

right: late-Gothic choir of the Church of Our Lady, 1404–30, in front of the choir is the low Baroque sacristy (1776) by Nikolaus Lauxen

CHURCH OF OUR LADY (LIEBFRAUENKIRCHE)

Located in the middle of the Old Town, this was the main parish church of Koblenz from the late Middle Ages to c. 1794. The present building had a number of predecessors, including a Roman hall church, which was refashioned in the fifth and sixth centuries to include an ambo and choir screen.

Construction of the present-day Late Romanesque church, a basilica with a vaulted nave and two aisles, started in 1180 and was completed in 1205. The present Late Gothic choir was added between 1404 and 1430 to plans by Johann von Spay (d. 1420). In about 1470, the nave was modernized by the inclusion of the magnificent rib-vault. The turrets surmounting the towers were destroyed in 1688 but replaced in 1693/94 by the archiepiscopal court architect Johann Christoph Sebastiani. This measure was followed by further Baroque alterations, which however were removed in their turn in 1852 by the Cologne cathedral architect Vinzenz Statz, who replaced them by neo-Gothic and neo-Romanesque elements. The most important thing to see in the interior today is the winged altarpiece by a Flemish master depicting the Adoration of the Magi (1584, in the choir).

The effect created by the galleries and the high clerestories is unusual. The triforium gives the nave proportions which come across as very lofty. The original Romanesque choir now forms the transition from the nave to the somewhat broader, aisled Late Gothic choir.

Church of Our Lady, twin-tower façade (top), plan (bottom right), interior view looking towards the choir (p. 23), tomb-stones of Reinhard von Burgtorn (d. 1517) and his wife Guta (d. 1553) in the vestibule (bottom left)

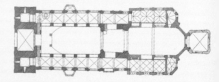

Nikolaus Lauxen, and by the former Jesuit College, which now serves as the City Hall. After the Jesuit order had settled in Koblenz in 1580 during the Counter-reformation at the behest of Archbishop Jakob von Eltz, using the buildings of the Cistercian nuns who had moved elsewhere, the first new buildings were erected from 1588/89 (starting with the south, and followed by the west wing, under the direction of Georg Monreal); the imposing church, with its galleries in the post-Gothic style with Renaissance ornamentation was built in 1613–1617. The church was destroyed in 1944, and only the 1617 façade with its splendid rose window and portal was rebuilt, while the main body was constructed to a new design by Dominikus Böhm in 1958/59. The stained glass is by Jakob Schwarzkopf (1962). The pilgrimage picture dates from the fifteenth century. The part of the college facing Jesuitenplatz was built by Johann Christoph Sebastiani in 1694–1701, the tower helms are by Johann Georg Judas.

Jesuit Church, façade – portal with John the Baptist (patron saint of the church), Ignatius of Loyola (founder of the order) Francis Xavier (Jesuit saint) and Archangel Michael – and interior

JESUIT COLLEGE/ CITY HALL

Jesuitenplatz, with the statue of the anatomy professor Johannes Müller (1801–1858), a native of Koblenz who researched among other things into the clotting of the blood, is dominated by two Baroque houses with dormers dating from 1773 by the city architect

left: 'Schängel' Fountain by Carl Burger, 1940. The urchin Schängel spews water every two minutes. 'Schang' is derived from the French 'Jean', and 'Schängel' ('Johnny') was a nickname for a Frenchman during the period of French occupation and also a generic name for all boys (today girls too) born in Koblenz
right: Jesuit College
bottom: Jesuitenplatz with the memorial to Johannes Müller

RHINE EMBANKMENT

The Rhine embankment is dominated by the monumental buildings of the 'Coblenzer Hof' hotel (1911–13 by G. Müller-Erkelenz) and the neo-Romanesque administrative building, based on the palaces of the Hohenstaufen dynasty (1902–06 by Paul Kieschke); this once housed the offices of the Prussian administrative region of Koblenz.

right: History Column (1992) by Jürgen Weber on Josef Görres Platz. Above the Roman wine ship, the history of Koblenz is told in pictures: Roman town, Frankish royal court, destruction in 1199, Crusades, heyday in the Middle Ages, Thirty Years' War, French Revolution 1789, 19th century, Second World War, and today
bottom: 'Wine Village' – goes back to the Reich 'German Wine' Exhibition of 1925

top: Rhine embankment with former government building (today the Federal Office of Defence Technology and Procurement) of 1902–06 and the 'Coblenzer Hof' hotel of 1911–13, with the Rhine crane in front, constructed in 1609–11 to plans by Peter Werner with the help of the fortification master from Jülich, Johann Pasqualini

middle: Regierungsstrasse 7, former customs office and official residence of the regional administrator, today the regional court building, c. 1906 by Paul Kieschke

25

ELECTORAL PALACE

The Electoral Palace (1776–92) by the architects Pierre Michel d'Ixnard and A. François Peyre jun. on the Rhine embankment was one of the last monumental palace buildings of the eighteenth century and at the same time the first and most important early neo-Classical building in the Rhineland. The Rhine front measures a stately 160 metres in length.

The palace was commissioned by Archbishop-Elector Clemens Wenzeslaus von Sachsen. He decided to build the new residence to the south of the city (replacing the Philippsburg in Ehrenbreitsein), with a view to encouraging the building of a satellite new town there. As the elector had to flee the advancing French revolutionary troops in 1792/93 and was finally expelled in 1794, the interior was left uncompleted. The palace has been put to various uses in the intervening period. In 1842–45 some rooms were refurbished in the neo-Classical style by Johann Claudius von Lassaulx to designs by Friedrich August Stüler. From 1845 to 1918, the upper floor was a residence of the Prussian royal house, while from 1846 to 1911 the ground floor housed the offices of the administration of the Rhine Province. The palace was destroyed in 1944, but some of the fittings were restored.

Stresemannstrasse 3/5 (next to the Palace), former government headquarters of the Rhine Province, today home to a planning authority, 170 metre long show building dating from 1907–10 (architects Saran and Bohnstedt) on the model of Franconian and Rhenish Baroque palaces

St Joseph, 1895–98 to plans by Josef Klee-sattel, very high-quality neo-Gothic building as the focal point of the southern suburb with a 90 metre tower and original fittings

DEINHARDPLATZ

At the focus of the late-Baroque city extension is Deinhardplatz, named after the headquarters, built in 1786, of the Deinhard wine business, then the centre of the trade in still and sparkling wines (since 1969 the Deinhard Cellar Museum).

The centre of the square is occupied by the fountain obelisk of 1791. The City Theatre was built as a prestige edifice by Johann Andreas Gärtner in 1786/87. The neo-Classical auditorium is worth visiting. Next to the theatre is the 'Trierer Hof' hotel, built in 1786 by Christian Trosson.

Deinhardplatz with the original Deinhard store (now the Deinhard Cellar Museum, left), the City Theatre (middle), the 'Trierer Hof' hotel (right), and the Fountain Obelisk of 1791

Sacred Heart Church, 1900–03 by Ludwig Becker, picturesque church in the style of Rhenish late Romanesque in a prominent position on the Friedrich Ebert Ring, fittings destroyed in 1944

KOBLENZ-EHRENBREITSTEIN

EHRENBREITSTEIN FORTRESS

The right bank of the Rhine (Koblenz-Ehrenbreitstein) is dominated by the majestic Ehrenbreitstein Fortress, which stands atop the steep cliffs opposite the mouth of the Moselle at an altitude of 118 metres. It is one of the strongest fortress complexes in Europe.

The land in front of the fortress was the venue in 2011 of the Federal Garden Show. The **Rhine Cableway**, Germany's longest, connects the left bank, next to St Castor, with the fortress plateau. It can transport up to 7,600 people per hour.

Ehrenbreitstein Fortress, ground plan

Ehrenbreitstein Fortress houses the **Landesmuseum Koblenz** in the Hohe Ostfront building (with special exhibitions, most recently 'Peter Joseph Lenné – A Garden Trip through the Rhineland' and 'My Final Garden – 10,000 Years of Funerary Culture on the Rhine and Moselle') and further exhibition buildings: the '**House of Archaeology**' (in the 'Contregard' to the right), the '**House of Photography**' (in the 'Nameless' Tower), the '**House of Food and Drink**' (Lange Linie) ('Wein-Reich Rheinland Pfalz', an exhibition of the wine culture in Rhineland Palatinate) and the '**House of the Poignard Collection**' (with objects reflecting bourgeois lifestyle from the eighteenth to the twentieth century). The '**Fortress History Trail**' takes visitors around the complex and at the same time explores its past. The fortress is also home to a youth hostel.

A first castle is said to have been built here c. 1000 by one Erenbert from the noble Konradin family. Not long afterwards it passed to the Archbishops of Trier, who continually expanded the complex. As it was regarded as the most secure place in the archdiocese, it was here that from 1380–1422, a precious relic, the head of St Matthias the Apostle, was kept. In around 1500, work started on extending the fortress on to the plateau to the north. The complex attained its present dimensions during the seventeenth century. Even so, in 1799 French troops succeeded in taking the previously invincible castle after a siege lasting more than three years, starving out the archbishop's defending forces. In 1801, it was razed. The new fortress took shape from 1815 to 1832, borrowing elements of the Baroque complex, but using modern design and technology. Its present appearance dates from this time.

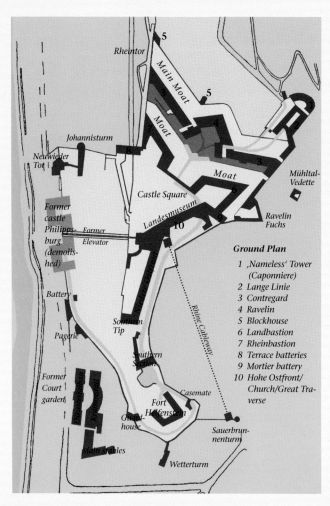

Ground Plan

1 ‚Nameless' Tower (Caponniere)
2 Lange Linie
3 Contregard
4 Ravelin
5 Blockhouse
6 Landbastion
7 Rheinbastion
8 Terrace batteries
9 Mortier battery
10 Hohe Ostfront/ Church/Great Traverse

Ehrenbreitstein Fortress, view from Pfaffendorfer Bridge (Rhine bridge)

top and bottom: Ehrenbreitstein Fortress

ELECTORAL BUILDINGS

Beneath Ehrenbreitstein Fortress, there originally stood the Electoral Residence, built by Archbishop of Trier Philipp Christoph von Sötern in 1626–29 to plans by Georg Ridinger, and named Philippsburg after himself. Following the completion of the Electoral Palace in Koblenz (see p. 26) in 1786, the Philippsburg stood empty. It was blown up by the French in 1801, and the remains were demolished not long after. What survived were the stately ancillary buildings, which are imposing enough in themselves: to the north, the '**Pagerie**' (fortified gatehouse, 1690–92 by Johann Christoph Sebastiani), the long, palace-like '**Dikasterialbau**' running parallel with the Rhine, which housed the electoral administration (1739–49 to plans by the famous architect Balthasar Neumann), and behind it the '**Krummstall**' (also by Neumann 1744–47, a utility and stable building), and to the south the **main stables** (1762 by Johannes Seiz, Rococo portal decoration with masks and a rearing horse with a groom, 1762/63 by Joseph Feill).